MICROGRAMS

JORGE CARRERA ANDRADE

MICROGRAMS

TRANSLATED BY

ALEJANDRO DE ACOSTA

AND JOSHUA BECKMAN

WAVE BOOKS

SEATTLE & NEW YORK

Published by Wave Books www.wavepoetry.com
Originally published in Spanish as *Microgramas*,
Ediciones "Asia América," Tokyo, 1940

Wave Books titles are distributed to the trade by
Consortium Book Sales and Distribution
Phone: 800-283-3572 / SAN 631-760X
This title is available in a limited edition directly from the publisher
Library of Congress Cataloging-in-Publication Data
Carrera Andrade, Jorge, 1903–1978.
[Microgramas. English]
Micrograms : preceded by an essay and followed by
a selection of Japanese haiku / Jorge Carrera Andrade ;
translated by Alejandro de Acosta and Joshua Beckman.
p. cm.
ISBN 978-1-933517-55-1 (alk. paper)
1. Epigrams. 2. Haiku—Translations into English. I. Acosta,
Alejandro de. II. Beckman, Joshua, 1971– III. Title.
PQ8219.C27M5313 2011
861'.62—dc22 2011008122
Designed and composed by Quemadura
Printed in the United States of America
ACKNOWLEDGMENTS
The translators wish to thank Diego de Acosta,
Samantha Zighelboim and Jonathan Way. Thanks to
Loaded Bicycle for publishing some of these poems.
9 8 7 6 5 4 3 2 1

TRANSLATORS' INTRODUCTION

Jorge Carrera Andrade was born on September 18, 1902, in Quito, Ecuador, and died there in 1978, after spending the bulk of his adult life abroad. Carrera Andrade, who began publishing poems in his teens, spent his early career as a journalist and editor, before working as an ambassador to numerous countries, including the United States, Japan, and Peru. His distinguished literary career comprised a wide range of work, from editing and translation to criticism and poetry, much of which was published internationally and engaged international themes. For Carrera Andrade, the international was less about crossing boundaries and more about disregarding them in the name of the universal. He writes, "I try to testify to an ordinary man's orbit in time. At first he feels as a stranger in the midst of a changing world but later receives the visit of love and discovers deep within himself a feeling of solidarity with all men of the planet. In this sense I have traversed new countries in different latitudes and have returned to others already known, in a pilgrimage as passionate observer rather than as curious traveler." It is from this "worldly" perspective and influence that his work grew, and maybe the most fascinating of these works is his *Micrograms*.

Printed here as it originally appeared in the 1940 edition—part essay, part book of poetry, and part anthology—*Micrograms* creates, defines, historicizes, and presents a *new* kind of poem: the microgram. The microgram is a poem usually between three to six lines long and about little natural creatures (both flora and fauna) and their existence in the universe. Carrera Andrade creates a historic view of Spanish-language literature, through the lens of the Japanese haiku and the form of a European-influenced historic manifesto. While formally unique, it presents its newness with the gentleness and grace of a conversation on a shared idea. Using the most subjective of personal histories (few were as international) he sees and calls for an objectivity—a generous objectivity of the individual eye. He looks into longer works and there finds the shorter pieces that create the history for the microgram. Carrera Andrade sees the impulse for the microgram in much of the world literature he encounters. For instance, in his introduction to his Spanish translation of Pierre Reverdy, he writes, "The human warmth of a simple and hard life that arises from the entrails of Reverdy's work situates him exemplarily in present time, participating in collective joy and pain. He does not sing agonizing mythologies, nor does he dress up in mystical robes: his voice is that pure and simple poetry that escapes the ordinary—and also mysterious—life of men . . . Reverdy's technique is personal, and his greatest secret lies in the stripping away of all decoration: the cult of naked and simple expression."

Published in Tokyo in 1940, as Carrera Andrade was finishing a four-year stint as an Ecuadorian ambassador in Japan (and just prior to the publication of his translation of the poems of Reverdy), *Micrograms* is a presentation of many varied trajectories of attention meeting in a single simplicity of voice and vision. The book flows freely from a sort of subjective personal outline of influence, to a formal guide, to an anthology. Throughout much of his work, Carrera Andrade uses form as a guide to the process of being in and recognizing the world, and this process becomes through reading and writing the place from which he speaks. It would be easy to imagine that in this instance it is the Surrealist influence that prioritizes behavior and process over the finished reality of the poem, but that is because we often forget the real history of the haiku and concentrate on the simplicity of its form. We must remember that the history of haiku is that of groups and individuals considering the processes of living and creating indistinguishable, and meeting life with a rigid yet constantly available form. It is worth noting that Carrera Andrade created this manifesto not for an "ism" or movement, which by presenting its possibilities can easily find itself maintaining its limitations and borders, but for a form that, by presenting its limits, can focus on its possibilities.

In *Micrograms*, Carrera Andrade has harnessed a twentieth-century impulse and is scanning an earlier literary landscape and plucking out available bits for a new and specific history. As the world is populated by little creatures that are easily overlooked, so, too, is the world of literature populated. *Micrograms* is the recognition of an unseen history that becomes a real Latin American literary history as well as a celebration of the many hidden histories that only need to be imagined or presented. To identify a history is to create a history, and to create a history is to say that a history can be created. To create a form is to see a form and to share a form, but it is also to suggest that there is something in the world to be seen a new way.

ALEJANDRO DE ACOSTA
AND JOSHUA BECKMAN

ORIGIN AND FUTURE OF THE MICROGRAM

GENEALOGY

I do not pretend to have invented the Microgram. Already in Spain's Golden Age, Don Francisco de Quevedo y Villegas paused between two *Dreams* to write "Boda y Acompañamiento del Campo" [The Country Wedding Party] —a rustic chain of Spanish epigrams, grandfathers of the infant micrograms that I am releasing into the world.

In graceful quatrains of his typical humor, Don Francisco attempted a joyful caricature of the small beings of the garden: the radish, the onion, legumes. And then:

> Mrs. Artichoke,
> dressed like the thin:
> folds and more folds,
> little flesh and many skirts.

The microgram is but the Spanish epigram deprived of its subjective hue. Better: an essentially graphical, pictorial epigram. Through its discovery of the deep reality of the object (its secret attitude) it arrives at a refined emotional style. An epigram, then, reduced in volume, enriched by complex modernity, widened to every thing that makes up the vital chorus of the earth.

The classical epigram had a tendency to laugh. This one-sided character never satisfied those minds meditatively drawn to the spectacle of the world. It was necessary to add a transcendental sense to the humor: the vibration of life, the greatness of the message of small things.

To the playful schema of characters and events, one had to add the quick sketch that captures the gestures of insignificant lives, underappreciated by the contemplators of a monumental world. Thus was born the microgram.

EPIGRAM, *SAETA*, PROVERB, SONG

Once it escaped from the Castilian plateau, the epigram was drenched in mystical light. It twisted in tortuous

Arabic-Andalusian grace and became *saeta*. The *saeta* is the elder daughter of Spanish popular song. Wine and guitar go hand in hand with the birth of this song. When the wine cellar overflows with its regular crowd, the barrel taps sing out their liquid chorus. One can clearly make out the flutelike sweetness of muscatel, the tremolos of malaga, the dry hiccups of sherry, and the rough call of manzanilla. From tables encircled by olive-toned faces (with Cordobés hats and sideburns like the muzzles of blunderbusses), a metallic lament of guitars suddenly arises, and a spiraling voice begins to unleash in shreds every sob enchained in the caverns of the chest:

> The earth already swallows her.
> And I, who am an evil man,
> have yet to die of sorrow.*

The *saeta* has an even more tortured style, more of a racial inheritance. The spinning movement of the bayadère (dancing girl) to the monotonous beat of the drum in African

* From a poem by Juan José Domenchina.

cities—accumulations of lime quadrilaterals—is the same movement that accompanies the flutes, drums, and oboes of the Andalusian Easter. Only now the voice is the stylized bayadère. The body kneeling at the feet of the opulent Virgin of Macarena undergoes a sort of ecstasy, while a cry climbs the throat, between precise contortions, becoming a mystical howl.

Andalusian poets have taken up this lofty racial murmur in their creations. Fifteen years ago, Manuel Machado saturated our language with songs smelling of verbena, orange blossoms, cloves, and the oily hair of the Gypsies. Antonio Machado, who drank in the bitter Castilian light in the austere landscape of Soria, has also written proverbs and songs. The spiritual physiognomy of the late poet was that of a provincial schoolteacher before a desolate landscape made up of a stone fountain, four poplars in a row, and a circle of singing children. In *Canciones de varias Tierras* [Songs of Several Lands] Machado used pins of light to ignite brief poetic thoughts. Hinting at philosophy, in their substance and form they are true micrograms:

1

By the black water
Smell of sea and jasmine tree
Malagueñan night.

2

He sings sings sings
beside his tomato, the
cricket in his cage.

3

Among the black oaks
there is a stone fountain
and a little mud pitcher
that is never filled.

THREE EXAMPLES

Despite their stylistic differences, today's poets, such as Juan José Domenchina, Jorge Guillén, and Angel Lázaro, all write synthetic poems. Lázaro is the inheritor of the Spanish Romantic tradition, the dead poetry of the cocked hat and the pipe, in the margin of literary schools that have succeeded each other parallel to the advance of culture. In his *El Molino que no muele* [The Mill That Does Not Mill], the Orensian poet gives us a handful of emotional white flour and a glass of aged Galician sweetness. The poet's familiar landscape is the Lonia highway, the Pazo de Velle, and a rose garden where a boy gets lost; he is not under the quince tree, nor in the pigeon-shed, nor at the edge of a fountain,

> nor behind the rabbits
> as white as milk
> with a little red ball
> of crystal in their temples.

The Galician poet amuses himself, sketching these lines with the simplicity of childhood:

GAZE

> O child's gaze
> perfect microscope

able to see things in their exact size
and their true color

AIRPLANE

Aluminum butterfly
prisoner in lantern
looking for an exit.
She chokes . . . tires out.
God, lift her punishment!
Let her escape.

I have already spoken of the poetry of Jorge Guillén. I said that its metallic hardness, cohesion, tenacity, and rigor are increasing. I have already spoken of how his poetry's color is "the inside color" and how he is getting ever closer to the marrow of things. I must add that Guillén, more than anybody, knows the ways in and out of the Gongorean labyrinth, and that nobody else has so neatly captured the melody and light of Góngora's poetry:

Oh moon! So much April!
How vast and sweet the air!

Everything I lost
will return with the birds.

Summit of delight!
In the air everything is bird.
The immediate looms
resolved in distance.

The much-discussed Juan José Domenchina, master of a poetry rich in red blood cells and great vociferator in pages of ideological battle, has also been seduced by the compressed poem in *La Corporeidad de lo abstracto* [The Embodiment of the Abstract]. Familiar with the itineraries of the new poetry, he has not hesitated to call his collection of synthetic verse haiku, leaving behind the epigram, the proverb, and the song.

This is Domenchina's rain:

Summer rain:
in the green trees
hanging nests.

And this bird, masterfully sketched:

Dead bird
what feathered agony
in silence.

Another suggestive microgram:

What is dew?
Happy miniature
of my own home.

THE SUBTERRANEAN CURRENT

Spain is a tableau of many-hued beauty. Geographically, it is almost an island: it has beside it two watery seas, the Mediterranean and the Cantabrian, and that other sea of solid waves, the Pyrenees. Each region is a varied and complex whole. Each province is a perfectly demarcated and original world, where one may see the best specimens of men, animals, and plants. Every city is a cosmos. I do not agree with Ehrenburg, who went only to see the mules and mule-drivers of Castile and to speak with the anarchist

Durruti in Barcelona. I would rather be carried away by the deep melodies of Spanish popular song and read poets of ethnic features and olive-toned pigment, such as Rafael Alberti. He extracts fragrant drops of songs and *soledades* in his *nanas* [lullabies], in which sea breezes converse with land breezes—breezes of that earth that the Guadalquivir divides with its scimitar of liquid silver light.

The Granadian García Lorca uses scraps of songs and *saetas*, like multicolored wings, in the glazed-tile columns of his romances, more beautiful perhaps than the great medieval romances. Nobody can thread a needle of eternity with popular melodies like he can:

In the black moon
of bandits
the spurs sing out

Little black horse,
where are you taking your dead rider?

And these brief poems, already precise micrograms:

EARTH

The girls of the breeze
pass by with flowing trains.

AGAVE

Petrified octopus.
You put ashen ribbons
in the belly of mountains
and astounding molars
in the ravines.
Petrified octopus.

What's more, Federico García—creator of Antoñito el Camborio and the Amargo of that unforgettable *Escena del Teniente Coronel de la Guardia Civil* [Scene of the Lieutenant Colonel of the Civil Guard] that, years later, under the slim trees of Granada, cost him his life—was seduced at the end by the green and luminous wink of the Caribbean Sea. He got some fresh air under the coconut trees of Cuba and beneath the skyscrapers of New York. On the hunt, then, for the new rhythm, for the authentic music of the rumba that accompanies the noise of drumsticks and hard seeds that resonate within the small, hollow gourds moved to the beat by black hands.

Popular music, the melodies involuntarily intoned by streets and plazas, marketplaces and taverns, once transformed by the magic of the new art of our poetry, are truly insuperable as expressions of a people and of a race. The cry of the peddler in the great cities, the intonation of the local dialects, mechanical sounds, autochthonous songs and instruments are all called upon to enrich today's poetry. Even the poets who try to evade completely the real world that collides with and pushes us—that, despite ourselves, humiliates and uplifts us—cannot avoid the way that the thin melody of popular song slips in through the cracks in their poems.

MEANING OF THE HAIKU

We have found three relatives of the microgram: the Spanish epigram, song, and *saeta*. We must add one more: the

Japanese haiku, exotic brother arriving from the lands of rice and dwarf pines.

Spring showers make the peasants cover themselves with straw overcoats; flowering plum trees light up the air like candelabra; and young women wear light-colored kimonos. The landscape is sweet and youthful, like a porcelain field. Namiko-san in his paper house (unforgettable Kenjiro Tokutomi in my mother's library!) feels the shipwreck of his heart in a wave of strange perfume moving in from the horizon. It is the best time of year for the flowering of haiku in all Japan.

The haiku is a small lyrical composition, of but three lines, in which one tries to encapsulate an original concept of existence. A poetic thought. A philosophical meditation. It belongs to the family of the proverb, except that it must have a beautiful form, a poetic structure.

Bashō, who lived three hundred years ago, may be considered the true father of Japanese haiku: his vast and varied work, accomplished during his unpredictable wanderer's life, has yet to be improved upon. However, his disciple Issa, who has been quaintly called "the Saint Francis of haiku," deserves our preference for his love of small beings and the eternal dimension of his images, pregnant with philosophical maturity.

In our time, the master of haiku is without a doubt Kyoshi Takahama, whose compressed poems recently appeared in French translation with a preface by Paul Valéry. The author of *Variété* affirmed: "These small pieces are the size of a thought . . . Sometimes this thought graciously reduces itself to an expression of such absolute simplicity that it can almost be confused with a shudder, a murmur, or a passing perfume in the air."

The primordial rule of the haiku, according to Takahama, is that it must be inspired by the physical changes and the sentimental nuances that the cycle of seasons impresses upon the universe. In this sense there can be no true haiku without *kidai*, the feeling of nature. Kuni Matsuo explains that to understand the rule of *kidai*, as stated by Takahama, one should study the Japanese poetic tradition and the mollifying influence of Buddhism. In my own travels in the Far East, I have been able to observe the philosophical attitude of the Japanese, peasants and city dwellers alike, before natural phenomena, their way of contemplating "the instability of things and of human life with a complete quietude of the soul."

The haiku is a brief poem of seventeen syllables distributed in three lines: five syllables, then seven, then five. It might seem almost impossible to enclose the great movements of the universe in such a narrow space. But through a kind of magic, the poet manages to make the infinite enter into that small cell. There, every surprise may fit. The finest successes of technique are to be found in certain ancient or modern haiku. Above all, imitative harmony is an element that is rarely lacking and that can produce unexpected effects, as in Bashō's little poem:

> Furu-ike ya
> Kawazu tobi-komu
> Mizu no oto.

Which in our precise language means:

> Into the old fountain
> the frog jumps quick
> the water sounds.

The last line of this popular haiku emerges from Japanese lips with a lengthened modulation: *Mizuuu nooo oto.* From the prolonged vowel sounds a liquid resonance is loosed, like that of water opening up in concentric circles when struck by a foreign body.

TRAJECTORY OF THE HAIKU IN LATIN AMERICA

How did the haiku arrive in our America? It is a matter for patient research. We know that a taste for Asian evocation already existed in Mexican lyrics in the time of Gutiérrez Nájera, that disquieting Duque Job who wrote some of his best poetry—it is called *The Garden Mass* or some such—in a succession of epigrams of a pure and modern flavor. Later José Juan Tablada, one of the greatest Hispanophone poets, published his *Nao de la China* [China Boat], producing the best haikus yet written in our tongue. His poem "Peacock" has already been translated into several languages:

Peacock: a long glint.
Like a parade through the democratic henhouse
you pass.

His "Insect" brings to mind one of Germaine Beaumont's most suggestive poems in *Disks*, which compares a beetle with the "Brugnant Christian":

Little insect you go walking
wings folded at your sides
like the saddlebags of a pilgrim.

We must also mark another great signpost in the Latin American poetic geography: the Guatemalan Flavio Herrera. Herrera's eye, receptive and colorful, imprisons, with the stroke of an arrow or an emotional fishhook, the beings of the earth and sea. He mounts them, like living trophies, in his lyrical pages.

Held by one wing, here is the sparrow:

Unruly rascal.
Little motor flying
on a needle's point.

And the lime exhaling its aroma:

In the garden, its
yellow nakedness reverberates
in a bulging navel.

These are already perfect micrograms. As equally are those of Gilberto González Contreras, who has honored me with some formal variations on my poems. ("Influences," said to me one of those critics of twisted gaze that are found in my land, "influences of Flavio Herrera can sometimes be seen in your verses." Good friend, note this date on your cuff: my micrograms were finished well before 1927 and published in 1930.)

In the brief *Muestrario del Trópico* [Sample-book of the Tropics] by the Colombian Umaña Bernal, one finds a series of little poems in four lines, living poetic snapshots that may be called authentic micrograms as much for their intention as for the fine exactitude of their coloration. The banana tree, shaking its curves and great leaves like green machetes, the parrot and the tiger, night that launches the lunar harpoon, brambles dressed like beggars, all assume a magic life in this lyrical parade of things and beings.

The multifaceted, ingenious, and sarcastic Alberto Guillén has also written numerous compressed poems. But all those poems gathered in his rich and voluminous *Cancionero* are closer to the epigram and the witticism due to their individualistic and subjective character.

A GLANCE AT MODERN FRENCH POETRY

Epigrams, songs, *saetas*, haiku, proverbs, and poetic riddles. So many paths toward the synthetic poem. So many tiny perfume bottles in which to pour quintessentialized emotion. The newest literary schools, which crisscross their luminous signals all over the world, have not renounced the short poem; rather, they have lit a lantern in the midst of its mine of precious stones. If it is true that there is no longer the same fervor for the haiku that existed after the war, its cultivation has not been abandoned. It is ever more fresh and rejuvenated. Setting aside the first French haiku writers, such as Julien Vocance and Paul-Louis Couchoud, there are innumerable poets who pour their spiritual wine into tiny vessels.

Surrealism shows us a rich specimen collection of small jewels of grace and irony that may be likened to the microgram. Philippe Soupault sings, in brief poems, messages of the sky, the earth, and the bells that change their universal waves, of women that close farmhouse doors and men who drink slowly to the sound of the accordion. Marching arm in arm with Philippe Soupault are Ribemont-Dessaignes, Yvan Goll, G. Rosey, Benjamin Péret, and Paul Eluard, whose work has recently had an ecumenical resonance.

The Alsatian Yvan Goll is a cosmopolitan spirit. Restless, with a new wit, inventor of contemporary myths, an original witness to the modern world, he has sought to write an epic poem in the manner of Tasso or Klopstock. He has written the *Die Chapliniade* [The Chapliniad], whose hero moves us, with his bowler and his cane, among a chorus of mechanical images.

"In this century of cement and hypocrisy," writes Goll, "one must have radium eyes." "The sky is copper, pockmarked with burning cigars, in the city of automatic desperation." "The dawn descends in an elevator. London has never heard a cockcrow. It has no fountains in which to wash the heart. Jewelers display necklaces of tears. A new Jesus, sportier, crosses the street where Chaplin is born."

In his *New Orpheus*, the poet gives us authentic micrograms such as:

ACACIA

The summer explodes.
Who launched the
acacia bombshell?

Léon-Paul Fargue, François Mauriac, Francis Carco, and Blaise Cendrars also write small poems sharpened with a modern intention. Cocteau, too, who calls the rooster "harlequin of the summer." But the French poet of our time who has felt the greatest attraction for the microgram is Paul Eluard. His *Les animaux et leurs hommes, Les hommes et leurs animaux* [Animals and Their Men, Men and Their Animals] is a collection of tiny objective poems, perfect in form and color, like tiny stamps in a book of natural history. The spider, the dog, the chicken, and the horse are the heroes of these poems, among whom even the most vulgar and humble comrade, the pig, is welcome:

Sun on the back, sun on the belly
With his snout thick and
immobile like a cannon
the pig labors.

SOUTH OF THE SYNTHETIC POEM

Can one indicate the future itinerary of the microgram? Surely synthesis, novel images, internationalism, and a childlike quality, which are the characteristics of the new poetry, will contribute to its renewed and endless life. But the more we emphasize a simpler vision of the universe, the greater will be the future possibilities of the microgram.

The earth's skin has gradually begun to thicken with the works of men: tunnels, train tracks, buildings of all sorts. The metallic tower of the wireless telegraph is the tree of the modern eclogue. The waves and messages that cross intermittently in the sky have begun to replace birds. The "insignificant heroes"—as someone called the beings in my micrograms—will surely be defeated by the mechanical monsters that heavy industry is creating all over the world. The hummingbird, the snail, the macaw, the crickets are all concluding their festival of color and sound before the advance of the motor, that hurried heart of the twentieth century. But this does not signal the death of the microgram. It will be reborn, rather, adorned with an urban character. The hero will no longer be the oyster or the swallow, but any of those mechanical creations that are transforming our time into an Age of Steel. The new cosmogonic consciousness of life will extend from the country to the city, matrix of the new man. And the microgram, that tiny lyrical composition whose name only I have invented, will bloom again, more vital and suggestive than ever.

Then the shade of Don Francisco de Quevedo y Villegas, he of the sharp intellectual smile, he of the gaseous irony that seems to filter through his funnel-shaped goatee, will smile.

MICROGRAMS

1926—1936

ORDERING A UNIVERSE

There is a many-hued and ever-changing immediate universe, composed of small beings that our hand can move at will, placing them in a more or less harmonious order. In this little animated universe, which has surrounded me since childhood, I was able to mark my preferred friendships and give myself over to a kind of cosmic and nontranscendent—though meaningful—game.

In this way, to the hummingbird, which is a flying prism or something like the wandering spirit of colors, I gave the spider as a companion: a patient and moderate worker. Beside the clam, which is immobility itself, rough, unformed indifference, muffled up before the spectacle of things, I put the snail, which is a lesson, however timid, in effort and marching. I made the macaw of my Amazonian Ecuador light its paradisal fire, like a hope, together with the turtle, which is raw patience.

I united the good beings that express their happiness through smell or aroma with the stag that is the apprentice of mountain lightness. Of a lightness or speed that is a kind of perfume. For the crickets that observe a monotonous discipline of builders, I marked a place at the foot of the architectural palm tree, solid green waterspout of the tropics.

I discovered that ugly beings, too, in their own way, work at a lovely task, and that the toad, the blowfly, and the worm are so many other ciphers of the secret key of the universe. The animated snow of the flamingo, the vegetable misanthropy of the cactus, and the hidden work of the caterpillar in the tree led me, in an ascending cosmic scale, to decipher the alphabet of birds, signs on high that maintain the spiritual order of the planet.

HUMMINGBIRD

Hummingbird,
sunflower needle,

backstitches of pink light
made on a trembling stem

with the sugar thread
it pulls from the flower.

OYSTER

Two-top clam:
your calcium coffer
keeps the manuscript
of some shipwreck.

WHAT THE SNAIL IS

Snail:
tiny measuring tape
with which God measures the field.

MACAW

The tropics patch together
golds and fires to make for him
a coat of flags.

TORTOISE

The turtle in its yellow case
is the clock of the earth
stopped centuries ago.

Dented now it hides
among the tiny stones of time
in water's blue cover.

NUT

Nut: wisdom compressed
little vegetal turtle
magic brain
paralyzed for all eternity.

TYPEWRITING

Late Night Toad: your little
typings strike
the moon's blank page.

THE SPIDER

Floor spider:
epaulet
fallen from
time's shoulder.

BERGSONISM

In the alphabet of things
the snail invents
the penultimate letter.

From its little cell
before the spectacle of the world
it stretches out
its living Y.

Ypsilon,
the snail begs
continuity.

ZOO

Flamingo:
chalk pothook in a puddle,
movable flower of froth
atop naked stem.

THE EARTHWORM

Constantly tracing in dirt
the long inconclusive stroke
of a mysterious letter.

KERNEL OF CORN

Every morning
in the rooster's beak
each kernel becomes
a cob of song.

BLOWFLY

Blowfly: grape with wings.
On your raw sweet silence
the heart gets drunk.

SWALLOW

Anchor of feathers:
searching for land
in a sea of sky.

THE PEAR

The air string cannot
spin its green top.

CACTUS

Sharp cacti fire
their chlorophyll rockets,
scarlet explosions.

BUTTERFLY

Bandaged child,
when you unfold your wings:
living leaflet of the field.

POPLAR

The poplar dips its brush
into the sky's sweetness
and makes a landscape of honey.

DEFINITION OF A SEAGULL

Seagull: foam eyebrow
on wave of silence.
Kerchief of shipwreck.
Skyroglyph.

THE CORN

It is gold and silver, the laugh
of decapitated corn
on its high green pike.

ALPHABET

Birds are
God's handwriting.

PLATEAU DWELLER

Stag:
your eye is a bubble of silence
and your flowery horns are needles
for stringing together stars.

CRICKETS

Crickets plant their blue flags
atop the evening
with tiny glass hammers.

PALM TREE

More than a tree, architecture
borne by sun and wind,
the palm is the column
of the sky's arched window.

THE MOUSE

The mouse,
a workshop official,
makes paper
shavings.

Psst . . . the lordly *y*
and the *es* of books
he likes to spell.

FISH

Living pink tube,
the fish writes glass zeros
in the fishbowl.

LIZARD

Lizard:
silver amulet
or little devil with goiter,
creature of dawn.

Memory of ruins,
fleeting animated mine,
shudder of field,
misanthropic lizard.

PALM READER

Atop the lines of a leaf
the slow finger of the caterpillar
deciphers good fortune.

SUMMER MUSIC

In its embers, summer
is grilling a cicada,
intimate flesh of the tree.

SEASHELL

Among the sands,
the seashell,
memorial stone
of a fallen seagull.

CELESTIAL WORKER

A celestial miner
digs a wide passage
in the deep night,
bright star.

JAPANESE HAIKU

SELECTION AND

FREE TRANSLATION

Imprisoned beneath the leaf
an anemone watches
the world's sadness pass.

YAHA

With threads of pearl-barley
oh frog monk
I will build you a house.

CHIGETSU-NI

The cicada.
Nothing in its song reveals
that tomorrow it must die.

BASHŌ

Pepper of my soil:
Give it wings
and it is a red dragonfly.

BASHŌ

The coastal wind
disorders above the sea
the seagulls' wise drawings.

SORA

Closed house:
Around the paper lantern
the bats dance.

RANSETSU

Water connects the islands
crowned by pines:
Matsushima Sea.

HOKUSHI

Autumn's cicada
lies dead beside
its empty shell.

JŌSŌ

Beneath the vast snowfall
many hidden seeds
wait for spring.

INEMBO

Vast calm.
Into the stones
only the cicadas' cry goes.

BASHŌ

In this everything ends:
The skeleton of a fan
when the autumn wind blows.

OTSUYU

The dead leaf
landing caresses
the stone tomb.

RANSETSU

Higashi, the mountain,
like a body
beneath a sheet.

RANSETSU

Bereft of song,
already dry and empty
the dead cicada.

BASHŌ

Together with the nightingale,
since I am going, guard my house
Mr. Snail.

ISSA

Wild goose, wild goose
how old were you
when you first cut loose?

ISSA

Weighing just enough, a snowflake
lowers to the earth
the leaf of the gladiola.

BASHŌ

Sliced cucumber:
Its juice runs
drawing spider legs.

KIKAKU

Spring dies
and filled with tears
are the eyes of fish.

BASHŌ

Little sparrow of a humble caste,
step aside: Here to pass is
the great Mr. Horse.

ISSA

A NOTE ON TRANSLATIONS FROM THE JAPANESE: The final section of *Micrograms* is a collection of poems translated by Carrera Andrade from Japanese into Spanish. We chose to translate these poems directly from the Spanish without referring to any of the numerous translations into English (or to the Japanese, which we do not know). It seemed that doing this would help us create a more unified tone, consistent with the tone of Carrera Andrade's book. We also thought we would enjoy the experience. We are deeply indebted to the many translators who have given us the work of the great haiku poets, and we are certain of the presence of their influence here. To say that there are better-equipped translators for this work is an understatement; we did it in the hopes that, through these poems, we would present not only the originals but also Carrera Andrade himself, as a reader and listener.